THRIVING WITH STRESS

Dr. Frank Wood

West Chester, OH • Thriving with Stress Publications

Thriving with Stress
Copyright © 2016, Dr. Frank Wood
All rights reserved
978-1522905479

Thriving with Stress Publications
9078 Union Centre Blvd, Suite 350
West Chester, OH 45069
Phone: (513) 448-4076
Email: info@thrivingwithstress.com
Information: www.thrivingwithstress.com
Orders: www.createspace.com/5959107

Contents

Forward

Okay, I admit it. I was a doubting Thomas in the first degree. When Dr. Frank Wood (you'll soon be calling him Dr. Frank) approached me about hiring him to help our staff at Curiosity Advertising learn how to manage stress more effectively, I scoffed.

That's because Curiosity Advertising is a 50-person national advertising agency that works with some of America's most familiar brands. I confidently told him that this is the ad business and we eat stress for breakfast. I also explained that this business is the epitome of change and chaos and that the folks who make a career in the ad world naturally thrive on stress—otherwise, they wouldn't be here. "We don't need this stuff," I said, and I dismissed it in my head.

Then I received "the look" from Dr. Frank for the first time (and sadly, it would not be the last). It was a look of wisdom, experience and patience. It was also the look a teacher gives a student who is acting like an all-knowing idiot. That day, I was that idiot.

I paused, and at that moment, I really began to listen. Dr. Frank explained that the negative effects of stress exist in every company and organization, and that no matter how much I denied their presence, those effects were indeed very present and doing great damage at the company I cofounded and love. From the start, my business partner, Greg Livingston, and I had chosen to take on a paternal responsibility when it comes to the health and well being of our staff. We have worked hard to build a culture of curious and creative professionals at Curiosity, and doing the right things to promote trust and collaboration is near and dear to our hearts. Was it possible that my being a doubting Thomas was putting us all in harm's way?

Well, that day Dr. Frank established a beachhead, as they say, and our HR director Vicki Johnson and I decided to put a couple folks through the *Thriving with Stress* program as a test. The results were immediate and very positive. Those staff members reported back that the program really works and that they were experiencing more positive interactions with their peers. Some even volunteered that *Thriving with Stress* actually improved life at home since they were better able to communicate with their spouses. One person said that for his entire career people had told him to stop certain behaviors when he was under stress, but we were the first people to actually help him learn how make the most of the situation and manage himself despite the stress. That's pretty heady stuff in my book.

Soon we began adding more participants. Then Greg and I figured we'd better volunteer to go through TWS, and that's when things really began to change—for the better.

I have to point out that *Thriving with Stress* is not rocket science or some kind of magic black box that instantly and secretly transforms people. It's also not a form of self-help therapy. It is a straightforward and easy-to-implement concept that helps you understand what stress responses feel like in the moment. With that knowledge, you can uncouple the emotional crap from the actual problem you are facing. In this book, you will learn that stress is like the wall between you and the solutions you seek. *Thriving with Stress* teaches you how to easily go around, over and under, but not through the wall. The big "Aha!"

So what did I learn about myself? I went in thinking I'm perfect and everyone else is not. Sound familiar? I quickly learned that no one is immune to stress, especially me, and that many of my hardwired responses were actually hurting me and making me a less effective leader. I take pride in being quick with the answer to difficult problems, and I always thought this was a positive character attribute and a big strategic advantage for me. I learned (a humbling experience) that what I had previously thought was a positive also had the potential to be a big negative and actually make "the work" harder for me AND the senior managers who report to me. I learned that my desire to get stuff done fast and make decisions quickly is a direct response to the anxiety I feel in stressful situations. I also learned that if I want Curiosity to grow and flourish, it is vitally important for me to sit on my hands and shut my mouth in order to give others around me time to solve the problem or deal with the situation effectively, instead of reacting with stress to my stress reactions. Makes sense right? Don't worry, it will.

Anyway, I am able to do this now by using the simple and effective methods Dr. Frank taught me, and these easy-to-understand concepts are now available to you in this book. Now the caveat: My "self-

As for Curiosity and *Thriving with Stress*, everyone has gone through the training. In fact, many people who witnessed the positive change in those who had completed the training actually volunteered because they saw it as something positive, helpful and good. As a result, we are growing and flourishing. Morale has never been higher and communication within the organization has never been better. My business partner and I resolve our differences without the disruption of stress, and we are focused on scaling our business with confidence.

So, spend some time with Dr. Frank. I promise you will not regret it. And if you have any questions about how a doubting Thomas like me became a big fan of *Thriving with Stress*, give me a call on my cell phone (1-513-236-5525) and we can talk about it, because I believe in Dr. Frank.

—Matt Fischer,
President and Chief Creative Officer,
Curiosity Advertising

Doctor's Note

My name is Dr. Frank Wood, but you can call me Dr. Frank, should we ever meet. To be honest, I love meeting people, so much so that I decided to get my PhD to study psychology and the science of the human mind. What I awoke in the process of my education in psychology was the entrepreneur within me . In time, I combined the lessons learned and developed the model of stress that I share with you in this book.

Funny thing, when you earn a PhD in psychology, it means that you get to meet people in the process.

While working on my PhD, I met a lot of adults, some who lived in nursing homes and others who lived with a developmental disability. My day-to-day interactions consisted of my having lost of conversations with a variety of individuals and their families—in other words, people who were experiencing a difficult situation, while their families were witnessing a loved one experience a difficult situation, thus experiencing a separate yet equally difficult situation. Day-in, day-out I witnessed elderly individuals with cognitive issues (let's call it dementia) and their younger counterparts handle the pressures, demands, and expectations—you know, life stuff (some people might call this stress). What I found is that, despite such drastic differences in age, specifics of the situation, stage of life, and level of intelligence at the time, all of my clients experienced a very similar pattern. This is not to say they responded the same way; what I'm saying is that when situations demanded more than the individual's capacity, most would make this evident in their emotions and behavior. The individuals who I met and came to know and care for and their family would identify things like anger, anxiety, outbursts, and so on. We could even go as far as to call these outbursts "antics." To compound things, I also noticed a similar pattern evident in my family and friends. Then, naturally, I discovered this same response pattern in myself.

That's when the entrepreneur in me decided to map out the pattern—the pattern that *everyone* goes through (that means you, sometimes). Are you ready? I'm warning you, it's pretty sad. Okay, here it goes. When a situation demands more than a person can handle, that person goes into a stress spiral (you will learn later that I call this the stress-response *life cycle*). As a result, behaviors change, he or she acts out and turns inward. After the dust settled, most would return to being themselves—but at the same time there was a lingering, please-don't-bring-that-issue-up-again-ness that lurked in the air. Simply put, for most people, there's no rising above stress, there's only getting through.

That's human history, folks. Millions of years of evolution have led us here: flipping out and then giving an encore performance for the rest of our lives.

Needless to say, I was unsettled by this discovery. So I went to work.

From these experiences, coupled with school, mentors—both professional and per-sonal—and, of course, my experience in "doing" therapy, I decided that there is good news and bad news. But let's get one thing out of the way: stress is inevitable, it's inescapable, it's everywhere. It's one of the few qualities that bonds the entire human race. No one is immune: your children, your spouse, your boss, your neighbors, your best friend, and your dog all experience stress. This, however harsh, is not the bad news, this is merely a reality of being human. The bad news is that up until this point, common pieces of advice for people experiencing stress are to "take a deep breath" or "relax."

Other go-to remedies are "Just deal with it," "Man up," and from our friends in advertising, "Never let them see you sweat." Ugh. Terrible, all of them. I have an idea that's equally useful: bang your head against a wall. It's just as effective and you'll at least give the people around a good laugh. Actually, the good news is that I have a much, much better idea. You'll find out more about this idea when you read the book.

It's important to keep in mind that this book won't eliminate stress, because if I found a way to do that, I'd be on a private island in a private ocean instead of writing. Honestly, I believe seeking to eliminate stress is a fool's errand and claiming to do so is misguided. This book will help how you interpret the demands of your day-to-day life and empower you to move past the stressful situations, relationships, and challenges, and allow you to move on with your life. Trust me, if that sounds simple, it's because it is.

not to like. She was one of those people that people are drawn to. Having been surrounded by books most her life, she could speak to almost any topic. Ellen was sharp. A breath of fresh air in my professional life, as you could imagine.

One morning while Ellen and I were talking (psychologists might call this treatment, but I preferred to *talk* to those people who permitted me the opportunity), the topic of travel came up and she started to talk about her life—something she rarely did. Several years before, she and her husband promised one another they'd go to Ireland when he retired. She'd wanted to visit since she was a little girl, and her husband agreed it would be a nice way to cap off 40 years of working. The day came, Ellen's husband left work for the last time, his coworkers threw him a party—there was cake, balloons, well-wishing, the whole thing. Over the next few weeks they planned the trip of a lifetime. Tickets were purchased, bags packed, and to-do list of spectacular views and adventures was carefully curated.

Then he had a heart attack. The trip was postponed.

They waited, her husband eventually recovered. They waited some more, and then, 20 years later, her husband passed away. Neither of them ever made it to Ireland.

How terribly sad is all of this? Wait. Don't answer that question. The only acceptable answer is very, very, terribly sad.

I don't bring up Ellen's Ireland-less shuffle into oblivion without a reason. Ellen's story illustrates how a perfectly reasonable, likeable, smart, talented, interested person can still respond to stressful situations in the worst possible way. Her husband's heart attack—an obvious point of stress—threw them both into an unrecoverable spiral, despite the fact that her husband managed to recover from the incident physically. The heart attack delayed the trip, but their anxiety, fear, and irrationality is what cancelled it. If you stay with me, you can see that the initial reaction to the heart attack was anxiety, fear, or fill in the blank with the emotions you might add to that list. The decision to postpone the trip, well, that is what I call the stress response. We'll cover the difference between stress and the stress response later (did we already talk about this?). For now, back to Ellen.

What they needed was a plan, a framework to give them a go-to state of mind. Ellen and her husband needed Rampitude. I know that Rampitude probably sounds like an event at the X-Games to you right now, but in time I'm confident you'll come to find it's the word and concept that will save you time, hassle, relationships, and energy.

I refer to it as a framework because it's a way of looking at situations—a perspective that, ideally, reframes how we approach and address stress. Specifically, Rampitude is about the reality of situations and aims to reclaim the power that we've given stress over the years.

Rampitude is versatile. It can be a verb and a noun, depending on the situation.

1. **Rampitude *verb*:** To notice, appreciate, and use the gateposts (off-ramps) that exist between a place of settled calm and a destination of negative urgency.

2. **Rampitude *noun*:** a nonjudgmental description of a location on a continuum that spans from "I'm okay" to "I AM NOT OK!"

Interestingly, all of us follow the same stress-response life cycle. How the process takes form, what it looks like, and the thought processes and actions, vary from person to person. We are all unique. Our story is our story—how we see, process, and react belongs to us, so it only makes sense that a unique solution would allow us to be more capable, reliable, and effective. Rampitude is that unique solution.

Because Rampitude enables individuals and teams to more clearly identify how the stress response intersects with effectiveness, it helps people remain settled during times of demand, pressure, or stress, leading to increased capability to think and act with purpose.

You probably think this is the part where I tell you all about Rampitude and exactly how it's going to change your life, right? No way! That's not how books work. We have a lot to talk about, and it's mostly about stress, so buckle up!

Hero's Journey

We all have the potential to be heroes. I realize that sounds like something that would be printed on an inspirational poster written by your mom, but it's true. However, don't feel special just yet, I said *potential*. Now, when I talk about heroes, I'm not talking about a person with a cape who saves beautiful women, clueless children, and stranded cats. Those are superheroes and firemen. Different book. I'm talking about heroes in the literary sense—the ones we read about, whose stories we've heard again and again.

It's probably been a while since your last English Lit class, so let's brush up on the Hero's Journey. The Hero's Journey is a storytelling pattern identified by Joseph Campbell, an American scholar and writer. It looks like this:

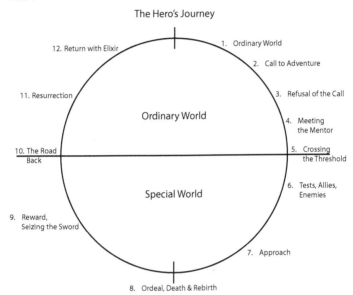

The Hero's Journey

12. Return with Elixir

1. Ordinary World

2. Call to Adventure

11. Resurrection

3. Refusal of the Call

Ordinary World

4. Meeting the Mentor

10. The Road Back

5. Crossing the Threshold

Special World

6. Tests, Allies, Enemies

9. Reward, Seizing the Sword

7. Approach

8. Ordeal, Death & Rebirth

The Hero's Journey can be found in most of the movies and books we consume—you're probably associating your favorite story with the above diagram right now while also wondering, "What does this have to do with handling stress?"

Fair question. Trust me, I'm getting to that.

Our brains are wired to be attracted to the hero's journey; we're drawn to it. So who's to say we can't have our own journey? Who's to say we can't make it all the way around the wheel?

I'll use a timeless, royalty-free example with which most people are familiar: let's call him Duke Groundrunner. Duke lives in a galaxy far, far away with his aunt and uncle on a dirt farm. One day, while toiling in the dust of his home planet, Duke receives a hologram message from a princess telling him that she needs help. This princess wears not one, but two buns in her hair. She's a bit much.

Are you with me so far? Good. Lawyers, am I in the clear? Good.

Duke's story has only just begun. According to our diagram, his hero journey has reached approximately 2:00. There are obviously millions of ways Duke's story can go, but for the sake of the argument let's just say it can go one of two ways. Duke can either go find the princess, embark on an incredible adventure, meet amazing people, learn, be tested, fail, succeed, learn some more, establish a belief system, fulfill his destiny and experience a full and rich life—or he can get worked up that there's a hologram of a princess, overthink his theoretical responsibility, and decide that moving dirt around would be a better use of his time, effectively stopping his journey at the starting line.

Believe it or not, most of us choose the latter. I have, you have, the whole world has at one point or another. It's maddening. We are called from our ordinary world to take life by the horns but we get stuck. We get stuck in our own mind and the behavior that this stuck-ness produces. You will learn later that your central organ of the stress response is your brain, and when it becomes confronted with a situation that seems dangerous (potential or real) your brain enters survival mode. We spin in circles until we're exactly where we started, having learned nothing, ready to get back in line to ride the ride once again.

We don't do this because we're self-destructive; in fact, it's the opposite; we operate best when our brain thinks things are safe. That's why we behave in a way to regain safety: because we're so concerned with ourselves—our own story—we fail to see situations and other people for what they are. We fail to appreciate their story or, to a much larger extent, the bigger, overall story. Ultimately, we fail to see reality. One of the biggest human failures is our inability to look outside of ourselves and understand and accept the reality of the situation—and in our case, the reality of stress. In a way, the things we are confronting may only be the start of a great journey, but more often than we'd care to admit, we opt to react in that moment instead of taking the bull by the horns.

This isn't a soapbox on the great tragedy of narcissism—narcissism is human. I'm merely setting up that the problem isn't stress so much as it's how we rattle (sputtering, stewing, fuming, raging, getting passive aggressive) and why we handle it so inefficiently. And how the more inward we go, the smaller our field of vision becomes, and the less productive we become.

Once we reframe how we respond, we can leave our dirt farms, say goodbye to our aunt and uncle, and become heroes just like Duke Groundrunner. All we need is a little perspective. A lot of perspective helps too, but for now let's start with a little.

Change

This book is about change. Of course, the trouble with that is we all run from change like it's Godzilla. We crave routine and we want what we know. There's absolutely nothing wrong with this: it's just the way we're wired, it's survival. We do this because we know the outcome of the decision— good or bad—and familiarity trumps reason.

Our love affair with routine influences more than we realize. It's what we eat, how we drive to work, where we like to sit around our table or on the couch; it's even evident in how we behave when we're meeting someone for the first time. For the most part, nearly everything we do in our day to day is done the same way. This is all harmless, of course, until it becomes a part of how we approach stress and we find that it doesn't work—but we keep doing it anyway.

When things change, you must respond to the demand, pressure, or stressful situation. Responding to this change is a challenge, and that's when you experience a stress response. While our individual stress response is unique to us, it is typically consistent from situation to situation. For instance, my friend Ttam (name spelled backwards to protect his identity) likes to offer suggestions. His business partner Gerg (again, backwards for ironclad protection) likes to ask approximately 1 billion questions. Other people raise their voices, some stay silent and do internal damage control, some of us run away—and the list goes on. Other than the fact that these responses are at times unproductive, they happen whether we're confronting a boss, a spouse, a child, or a friend, and they happen regardless of the situation.

Each of us learned to do our "thing" because it worked and helped us to effectively cope with the change. The guy who changes directions and runs away? He learned to do that because running away at one point in his life worked. Same goes for the suggestion person, the question person, and the raised-voice person. It's not always bad, but can you see how this behavior might plague your interactions, problem solving, and ability to look at your harshest critic, which is you. Shocking, I know.

Keep in mind, the moment stress stops will also be the last breath you take; stress is not a thing you can avoid. The situations that occur and the people involved change from day to day, so responding uniformly because it's what you've always done will not yield different results. I think it was Einstein who said, "Insanity: doing the same thing over and over again and expecting different results." It's comforting, yes, but it's unproductive. I hate to be the one to break it to you, but comfort and productivity are rarely bedfellows.

Change is necessary. More specifically, adaptation is necessary. Our lives are in a state of constant flux: we don't stay the same and neither does the world around us. Each stressful experience needs to be taken in, assessed, and responded to as a separate and independent issue. They are not connected; unfortunately life isn't that simple.

The reason we find change annoying is because it merely suggests improvement, it does not mandate it. It means we have to move, to see things differently, act based on what we find, and ultimately become better, happier people. Gross, right?

Change means learning, and as adults we don't especially like learning. This is because we think we already know everything we need to know. We've made it this far unscathed, so what's the point? Right? Ha! No, that's so wrong. You should've seen that coming.

Any time we're required to learn something new, our brain acts like you brought a muddy, stray dog into a clean house and ask/yell questions like "Where am I going to put this thing?!" and "We don't have room for this!" and "This dog doesn't match any of our furniture and now everything is covered in mud."

The point is, learning new things can make us anxious; yes, even you Ms. Important Business Executive or Mr. Successful Middle Manager who just got a promotion. This will not be easy; we're all set in our ways and it will take a conscious effort, but change we must.

Sounds fun, right? I thought so. Let's do it. Plus, we're in too deep now. I'd even go so far as to call us friends.

Okay, okay, all in good time. Let's just move along to the next chapter, shall we?

Your Brain

BREAKING NEWS: NASA has made a discovery—one that will change the way look the heavens forever. After volumes of research, a very complicated launch sequence, and a handful of light years in a spaceship, they've concluded that YOU are the center of the universe.

Well, you're the center of your universe, anyway.

Yes, it's you. The stars, the planets, and even the sun—for all intents and purposes—revolve around you. This is, in part, because the world as we know it, everything we experience, is filtered through the most powerful part of the human body: the brain.

Our brain is the gatekeeper of information and helps us interpret our world. Dan
Seigel suggests the brain is a time travel
machine as it has an ability to take in what is
happening, make sense of that current
based on our past and then immediately
help determine which particular action is
most appropriate. Oh, and it can accom-
plish all of this in a portion of a second.

Our brain internalizes, rationalizes, cate-
gorizes, and then has an ability to determine
a course of action that is most appropriate;
the amazing thing is how often our brain
makes that split second decision with remarkable accuracy. It's a very complicated
system that seems to make our life less
complicated. If our brains didn't work like
this we'd probably spontaneously combust
from trying to decide between farm-raised,
grass-fed, or free-range eggs at the grocery
store.

However, our mind's constant filtering,
tagging, and storing is what leads to our
acceptance of reality as consistent, pre-

dictable, orderly (even though a permanent, unchanging elephant in the room continues to persist: the elephant could be a relationship, project, or any issue that plagues our brain). We talk to ourselves into accepting how we perceive reality as fact.

As a result, we commonly make sweeping generalizations about our own lives, other people, and the world without even realizing it: we keep drawing water from the same well. This is what forces us to arrive at earth-shattering conclusions about ourselves. Conclusions like "That's just who I am," or "That's how it's always been," or, my personal favorite, "If you can't stand the heat, maybe you should get out of the kitchen."

Classic stuff, really.

The large, all-encompassing implications of telling ourselves "this is the way it's always been" is that we're unable to understand situations differently than we've always seen them.

As you will begin to see, this tendency plays into our relationship with things that are demanding, pressure packed, and stressful, and results in what I call a stress response.

We all have a stress response and, for most of us, our stress response is unproductive and, sometimes, destructive.

Can you take back control?

The short answer is yes.

The wonderful part about freeing yourself is that you're not as doomed as I've illustrated above. Sure, our reptilian brains are basically hell-bent on keeping us locked in destructive behavioral patterns, but we're not doomed. We can't be. I won't stand for it, and neither should you.

How We Change

As much as I'd like to tell each and every one of you that you're a snowflake and your behavior is unique and it's what makes you, you, I can't. To a certain extent, we're all hardwired the same way. The outputs are probably different, but the motherboard is pretty much the same from person to person.

The way in which we form habits has been studied ad-nauseam. Habits are actions performed without a conscious effort, and all of them—good or bad—follow the same three-step pattern: Reminder, Routine, and Reward. The reminder is the trigger that initiates the behavior, the routine is the behavior itself, and the reward is what we gain from performing the action.

To illustrate the three elements of our habit pattern, I'll use something we're all familiar with: a phone call.

The Reminder: Your phone rings. The ring acts as a trigger to remind you to answer your phone, prompting your behavior.

The Routine: When your phone rings, you answer it.

The Reward: When you answer the phone, you find out who is calling and why. Depending on the caller, this may not be a reward, per se. When the reward is a positive experience, you'll want to repeat the task the same way when the reminder happens.

Our tendency to rely on what we think we know rather than our real experience leads us into misreading what is happening based on (a) what has happened (b) what we think is happening (c) what we think will lead us to a place where we are confident and safe.

This reminds me of a recent client where the owners were battling with each other. Well maybe not battling, but there was a rattle that existed when these two gents engaged in leadership chess.

During times of pressure, one of the co-owners during times of pressure would often knee-jerk into a series of questions. The questions were creative, insightful, many times unearthed clear directions, but became a dreaded foe to his partner.

Partner #2, during times of pressure and demand, would offer suggestions. These suggestions were creative, also insightful, many times brilliant and useful in moving things along.

Partner #2 often became frustrated because he felt that his habit (offering a suggestion) was quite useful in moving things along, whereas Partner #1's habit (asking a question) only slowed things down.

What is important is that both these individuals were only displaying a well-trained habit—a habit that had worked very well for them.

As with Partner #1 and Partner #2, we continue to keep doing things that work for us. It's pretty simple stuff. We rely on what we know rather than real experience because we want to stay safe, and we think we know what's best. Sigh, yes, humans are about as complicated as a sea slug.

Trust me, this is good news, because it means we're not stuck in our ways—we're malleable, we can change! This means your go-to stress response is anything but set in stone; all you have to do is learn something new and recognize that it works.

This is easier said than done, but it's by no means impossible.

The 64th Problem

Everyone has sixty-four problems. It's a running list of uncategorized concerns and, quite frankly, they're often all over the place. Problems 1-63 are all interchangeable; You don't exercise enough, they gave you incorrect change at the deli, your bills are piling up. Switch money troubles for "do these pants looks okay?" and repeat.

Your daughter calls to tell you she's got a new boyfriend, tattoo, etc. Your doctor tells you that there is a need for more blood work. As you turn onto the highway, heading toward a meeting, you see the red tail lights of a traffic jam.

We're constantly greeted by these sixty-three problems and even when we've solved one, another replaces it.

The real challenge is the sixty-fourth problem. The sixty-fourth problem is that we don't want to have any problems at all. Truth be told, this is the only problem we should ever care about.

That was a lot at once, let's take a step back. Pretend for a moment that your spouse or child has a flat tire. They call you: they're standing in the parking lot of the local mall and tell you that the tire is flat and the car is no longer drivable.

Now, be honest, what would you typically do in this situation?

I'll tell you what you'd do, because it's what most of us would do. You'd ask things like:

How did it happen?

Was there anyone else in the car?

Was it raining?

Where were you going?

We are trained from the age of three to ask "why" questions. We want to determine what happened, how it happened, what series of events have conspired to leave us with (a) a skinned knee (b) a low grade on an exam (c) water in the basement (d) that flat tire, and so on.

In reality, the only thing that matters about a flat tire (well first that you are safe, your car is not in a dangerous location, pleasantries, really.) is fixing it. It doesn't matter what you hit, it doesn't matter where you were going. It just needs to be fixed. If you consider the sixty-fourth problem, you wouldn't have had any questions except for maybe "where are you?" and the problem would be well on it's way to being solved.

Details are sensational and interesting but not really all that useful.

A friend, named InSoo, has told me there's another way to see it.

Why do we do this? Why do we focus on the irrelevant, unsolvable, and uncontrollable aspects of the problem? It's because we crave safety, and safety, at times, means avoiding the actual problem at hand—so we avoid the reality of the situation.

As it pertains to stress, focusing on the sixty-fourth problem helps us tremendously. Imagine you're frustrated with your boss about something and you spend your energy thinking about how he or she makes more money than you and doesn't realize what an asset you are to the company; you are asking other people what they think of the situation. Sure, you'll eventually go back to "okay" but it's only after several unproductive hours, days, weeks.

The sixty-fourth problem is about seeing the reality of the problem. It's about getting out of your head and preventing your brain from creating a (more than likely) false narrative around your situation: a narrative that only takes us to an unsettled, unproductive place. By focusing our efforts on the sixty-fourth, which is "I don't want any problems." We engage rather than tiptoe.

Stress at Work, Stress in Life

It's time to look the monster in the eye. The beast on our backs, the "s" word in all caps: STRESS.

We've all been there, we've all done that. At home, at work, in our car, at the grocery store, we've responded to someone or something in a less than desirable way. As you're reading this, you're probably thinking about the last person/place/thing that stressed you out.

Well, don't. You'll have plenty of time to do that later.

The next couple of chapters are about stress—what it means, where it happens, and how we deal with it—because understanding stress is vital to managing it. Most people think they have a good handle on what stress means. "Oh it's when I get angry" or they tie it to a person or situation, "stress is running late" or "stress is my boss." Overall, they're not wrong, and a lot of people think it stops there. However, it's important that we put on our helmets with the flashlights attached and dig a little deeper.

Most people can relate to work-related stress. Stress at work typically occurs when there's a mismatch between the demands of the job and the resources and capabilities of the individual worker to meet those demands. You have a job to do but the resources necessary to optimally perform that job don't exist and you're probably worried that the blame will fall squarely on your shoulders.

How people, organizations, and cultures define stress varies. However, because most of us have experienced stress at work (and perhaps have brought it home with us a time or two), I think it's important to get the

NIOSH (The National Institute for Occupational Safety and Health) perspective on what stress means in the workplace. NIOSH defines stress as the harmful physical and emotional responses that occur when the requirements of the job do not match the capabilities, resources, or needs of the worker. Job stress can lead to poor health and even injury. Furthermore, on the basis of experience, and, what I can only imagine, tons and tons of research, NIOSH favors the view that working conditions play the primary role in causing job stress.

Ahem. Think about that.

NIOSH—the government agency that was built and designed to protect you from harm in the workplace—does not consider individual differences as important as the working conditions. This means that NIOSH focuses its energy and resources on having the employer change the working conditions rather than helping the employee manage their stress response.

AHEM.

This isn't a NIOSH problem—well, okay, it is a little bit—but it's a culture problem. We think stress is totally rooted in the environment. I tell you this to give you a perspective on how pervasive this common definition of stress is. When it comes to stress, a lot of us (including NIOSH) feel that when you remove the stressful environment, you remove the stress. That's not necessarily the case.

Like NIOSH, most of us think "stress" is a thing we need to control, contain, deny, or avoid—because, well, duh, that's just the best way to deal with any problem.

Right?

Eh, not really.

I've developed my own definition of stress (see: the introduction to a new framework that I developed to free those who learn and adopt this framework, otherwise known as this book). I like to think it goes further into where stress comes from and, in doing so, points toward a better solution than switching up the ergonomic chairs or moving to a cube with a window.

My Take on Stress

To tame the beast, you must first understand the beast. That's what my father would always tell me, although I think he was talking about hitting a knuckleball, and not stress, or maybe he was teaching me how to ask girls out—I'm not sure, but he was right. Now that I think about it, he was probably talking about my aunt, not you, Peggy.

Let's begin to understand the beast. Here's the thing: the term "stress" is not the issue. The real issue is the thing that Rampitude is all about: the stress response. The most important thing you need to know is that stress is a reaction to circumstances. Before any of us will accept this, however, we first need to be aware that this reaction actually happens. Once we're aware, the more likely we are to acknowledge that reaction when it happens and pause the stress response.

There is a life cycle to the stress response. This lifecycle takes us from a place where we are calm to a destination where we find ourselves in a rage or frustration. However, those places are just the beginning (your experience of settled calm) and the end (your experience of negative urgency) of your stress response. Every journey has a middle. In fact, the middle is usually the most important part.

As we learn to be aware of and appreciate the metaphorical path that exists between okay and not okay, we can then understand that just like any path, we can stop walking, or get off the road *before* we reach the destination, which, in this instance, is a place called Spazville.

When we notice our place on this path, we can choose to pull off. When we do this, we're given the luxury of time, we find that we have a readily available flexibility, we can bring out our own personal creativity, we gain an increased perspective, and with that change in perspective comes under-standing. And respecting the stress-response life cycle and shortening the duration of the stress response is the goal here, ladies and gentlemen.

When we reach a place of understand-ing, we are more likely to perform to our capacity. That means we will be more ef-fective (and take action, or say whatever we say that helps with the issue at hand) and more reliable (we do not engage in ac-tions that are unproductive).

The reality is that there are a variety of people in every organization.

Each person in an organization brings a unique and specific set of skills, talents, train-ings. This means that every person in your company has value that they can bring to meet the demands, pressures, and stresses that come.

What if each member of your team had the ability to perform to their peak? The CEO, the sales manager, the production supervisor, the administrative assistant, the new hire—all of them at optimal performance level. Everything would change for the better, that's what.

The reality of stress isn't the he said/she said; it's not even the situation itself. It's about making a conscious decision to take a step back, assess the direction you're headed, and prevent stress from engulfing the rest of your afternoon, day, week, what have you. You're not a victim unless you construct the narrative that you are one, to justify getting upset, retreating, getting sad, or whatever your go-to stress response may be.

Know that stress is not the issue: the issue is the stress response, and, more to the point, the stress-response life cycle.

The Stress Response

This is a story about parenting, pizza, and off-ramps.

A few years back, in the late afternoon on a Wednesday in May, my 13-year-old daughter asked me to take her to dinner. Those of you who have ever had a 13-year-old daughter know that this is the parenting equivalent of seeing Bigfoot riding a jet ski. So off we went to grab pizza. It was a popular neighborhood spot and a beautiful night so when we arrived there was a wait. I dropped my daughter off and told her I'd go park the car.

I parked, walked in, inhaled the pizza fumes and realized how hungry I actually was. My daughter said it was a 15-minute wait, as I'd expected. I found myself a sturdy wall to lean against while she pulled out her phone and did whatever it is 13-year-olds do with the most advanced technology mankind has ever known.

15 minutes passed.

20 minutes passed.

22.5 minutes passed.

I asked my daughter if she was sure that it was only a 15-minute wait. She said yes. I checked with hostess to see how much longer it would be. She scanned the list, reached the end, and told me that our names were not on it.

Hm.

I asked my daughter if she put our names on the list. She said no. She then mentioned that she'd learned about the wait time after hearing a family talk about their wait time. This could only mean one thing: she never gave our name to the receptionist at the popular pizzeria.

HM.

At this point, I was no longer feeling that sense of excitement about pizza as it was replaced with tenseness akin to a Mt. Saint Helens volcanic eruption circa 1980 (well not really, but you get the point). I couldn't begin to fathom a valid reason she wouldn't put our names on the list. And what rubbed sand into the proverbial wound was she showed like zero remorse in her forgetfulness on top of it. As my mind filled with a portion of rage, I began peppering her with questions about why she didn't give our name to the hostess. Confused, she told me I never asked her to do that.

Reread that last part: I presumed she knew something that I did not tell her.

I exploded (technically, I imploded), and we left the restaurant. Not completely lost in my frustration, I did place a second order of the pizza we would have purchased at a sister restaurant and as we drove from Pizzeria #1 to Pizzeria #2, I continued my inquisition of my daughter and her apparent lack of capacity to understand simple non-verbalized directives.

As I began to sputter, my voice raised a bit at my daughter for not being more like me. I did this fully aware that my daughter is not me and I am older than 13. Really mature, I know.

Now, for those who are reading who are reading and casting judgment and deeming yourselves so much more mature than I, I ask you to recall your last episode of "sputter?"

I went from a place of calm, happy, and excited to a place where I was petty, impatient, frustrated, and angry in approximately 37/100 of a second. And I hate to break it to you, but I'm not alone in taking that path: we've all been there. Maybe it was this afternoon, or yesterday morning, or when you last spent time with your in-laws.

This path, although a fast one, has gateposts that we travel past on our way from that place of settled calm to the destination where we feel a negative pressured urgency. Gateposts are the cornerstones of Rampitude—I call them off-ramps. For instance, in my pizza meltdown (no pun intended), one of these off-ramps would've been my mind flooding with thoughts about my daughter being a really smart and gifted 13-year-old, that she must have had a reason for doing what she did, and that I was a 47-year-old father seeking to set a superior example of my being the best dad ever. My path went from pride (that I was going to eat a meal with my daughter) to frustration, to anger, to impatience. It all happened so fast. What I did not think about was how my daughter might have been unfamiliar with the busy-restaurant-drop-off-park protocol. Again, because she was 13.

Understanding that these gateposts exist and beginning to learn of noticing them are the beginning of something incredible: you not freaking out. Later I will identify the first four of these gateposts, off-ramps, in my training (see *Thriving with Stress* training).

Of course, this takes time and effort, but there are some tools you can learn so you can recognize the off-ramps and use them to exit the express highway that leads straight to Stressylvania. Population: You.

Take a few minutes and consider some of your recent implosions (internal fuming at a direct report or a boss), or explosions (yelling (or a euphemism for "yelling" that helps you to save face at anyone and anything). If you'd been aware of the gateposts or off-ramps, you might have responded more effectively.

Some might be hearing that voice that sometimes talks to you. That voice is saying that it's going to be difficult to know what these off-ramps are, and even more difficult to notice them when then happen, and then extremely difficult to remember to notice them in the first place. If you have that quiet and persistent voice, the journey will not be easy. However, when you learn the off-ramps, life will become easier.

For now, let's dive deeper into why we respond the way we do.

Why We Respond Like We Do

I've mentioned it before and I'll keep mentioning it, because I believe it to be true: Since stress is unavoidable, it's all about how we respond to it, rather than pretending it's possible to eliminate it. (Remember the 63 problems.) Let's dig deeper into the response.

The real goal is to 1) Recognize that you experience a stress response and then 2) Shorten its duration. This gives you an ability to thrive during your stress-response life cycle.

When we find ourselves in situations our brains considers dangerous our response is adaptive. In other words, our brain's natural response is to react to what's happening in front of us. This is good and bad. It's good if you're lost in the woods and you come face-to-face with a bear, because your brain says "RUN RUN RUN" but it's not great for a disagreement with a coworker. It's bad, again, because bear attacks almost never happen, whereas the latter probably occurred this week.

Hans Selye, whose work has greatly influenced my own, identified four components of the stress response that are crucial to know and understand. I'll put them in a list: people are really into lists these days, right?

HANS SELYE'S TOP 4 COMPONENTS OF STRESS RESPONSE YOU REALLY NEED TO KNOW ABOUT:

1. **Increased Thoughts:** Our brain goes through a rolodex of thoughts that it thinks might help us make sense of the situation. This includes finding similar situations through memory, and remembering how we've dealt with it before—successfully and unsuccessfully. Our brain is doing its best to make these past

experiences relevant to the present situation.

2. **Increased Emotions:** Our emotions motivate our behavior. You behave differently when you're curious versus when you're nervous. When our brain deems a situation dangerous, these emotions are amplified and change faster than usual. Therefore the output (our response/actions) will be amplified as well. For example, you have a client presentation at 9 AM and your coworker, who is always on time, is nowhere to be found. You begin to worry that something happened—an accident, flat tire, pulled over—and you're worried that you'll be left to do the presentation by yourself. When your coworker arrives and he or she was simply running late, you switch from anxiety to anger, as if someone flipped a switch.

3. **Reactive Behavior:** You might think of this as the flight or flight response. When we encounter a situation our brain per-

ceives as dangerous, we have the tendency to react quickly. This is the part where we run from the bear.

4. **Increased Body Tension:** During a stress response, our body is wired to seek safety. We're able to respond quickly due to a complex internal reaction that includes the production of stress hormones and the internal flood of energy to some parts of the body. For instance, your lungs will push more air to your brain and your heart will beat a bit faster.

Thus, during a stress response, if you pay attention, you will notice the pressure in your chest, or hear your heart beating, or feel your face flush. This body tension is simply another indication that you are experiencing a stress response.

5. **Need to Expel Energy:** After a stress response has occurred and we're frazzled, we have a biological need to discharge the energy. This doesn't mean we run a few miles around the office park. It's

more about expelling energy through expression. Gossiping or venting at work, spending an extra 10 minutes in the conference to talk about how ridiculous that meeting just was, or even cheering at a sporting event are all ways we expel our stress-response energy.

The following aspect of the stress response was taken from a researcher named Peter Levine.

Levine noticed that at the end of a stress response, there was a tendency to shift to a state of "rest and recovery" and many animals naturally do that with gentle trembling, shaking, deep breaths, sweating, and sometimes more aggressive fight-reenacting behaviors. He called this process *discharge*.

These behaviors reset the nervous system to a pre-threat level of functioning.

Importantly, this discharge cycle appeared to be essential to recovery: experts repeatedly told Levine that if animals were unable to complete the discharge process, they would die.

You've probably experienced one or all of these at some point in your life—at work, at school, at home, walking across the street—more or less all over the world. These are all perfectly natural reactions and they're what are known as stress responses. Human beings have had them for as long as we've been wandering around the globe.

So, what happens when we're stuck with a series of stress responses that were designed to escape a mastodon stampede and we're left trying to shoehorn them into the minutia of office life? Well, we're out of luck, kind of. We die more of stress-related diseases than any other member of the animal kingdom. Robert Sapolsky, a neuroendocrinologist, researcher, and author, summed it up perfectly:

> Primates are super smart and organized just enough to devote their free time to being miserable to each other and stressing each other out. But if you get chronically, psychosocially stressed, you're going to compromise your health. So, essentially, we've

evolved to be smart enough to make ourselves sick.

This is a classic Catch-22, everyone. We obviously *have* to respond to stress in some way, but at times the way we're wired to respond might not be all that helpful, especially when the threat is only a perceived threat.

During a stress response, our bodies respond to the threat by helping us seek safety. In doing this, we release hormones like adrenalin and glucocorticoids which instantly raise our heart rate, energy levels, and some people's metabolism. Again, this is because our stress response was designed to literally survive, not mull over situations in our heads. Our brain interprets the question "Is my boss happy with my performance?" to "Are we going to have enough food to get through winter?" and our body responds accordingly. Sapolsky explained that we mobilize energy in our thigh muscles (you know, to prepare to climb over a mountain), our blood pressure increases, and we turn off all the nonessentials, like digestion and reproduction. At the same time, we think more clearly and our memory is enhanced. Theoretically, we are perfectly suited to respond to stress; the only problem is that it's physical stress, not the psychological stress we have the luxury of experiencing.

What does this all mean? It means that we are ill-equipped to muscle our way though modern stress and instead of solving problems efficiently we get heart disease, diabetes, high blood pressure, lose our memory, become impotent and, naturally, we get fat.

What's fascinating is that the spare tire of blubber around our midsection is (partially) a protective element that occurs as a result of our stress response. The body wants to protect your major organs and so the fat that settles in the midsection is actually adaptive, but it's not really helpful anymore.

The bottom line, according to Sapolsky is,

If you plan to get stressed like a normal mammal, you had better turn on the stress response or else you're dead. But if you get chronically, psychosocially stressed, like a Westernized human, then you are more at risk for heart disease and some of the other leading causes of death in Westernized life.

Here's the thing, the person who knows whether you are experiencing a stress response is—wait for it—you. You might want to begin to pay a bit more attention to this experience more often in your daily life. As you do, you'll come to further understand that you are responsible for you. The more you become aware and acknowledge that you have this stress response, the more you can take ownership of your response.

A New Framework

Whew. This is what we've been working toward. I'm so happy we made it together. All you have to do to get the Rampitude outline and explanation is purchase my second book.

Just kidding. Okay, let's do this.

To restate what I feel like I've said a trillion times already, we all follow a metaphorical path that takes us from a place of "okay" to that destination of "not okay"; from a settled state of calm to a place of negative and pressured urgency; from satisfied and happy to that moment of frustrated not happy. You've probably been there a time or two this week.

This journey happens because our brain is trying to answer a set of questions while experiencing a situation: Am I safe? Have I been here before? Is there anything I can do? Should I leave? Should I stay? Like we talked about in the stress-response chapter, we're always determining whether conditions are such that we should engage or disengage and do our best, then, to adapt. Our highest order of adaptive responses is resorting to language, the mid-tier response is thinking and determining what can be done, and the most primitive response is to freeze up like an armadillo on the highway. Whatever our reaction may be, it's performed out of habit. We developed this habit because we've had success with it in the past, even though it won't work every time. Up until now, that's who we are: we're reactors, performing the same routine every time. The problem is—and always has been—that we're just trying to survive instead of trying to thrive.

So here we are, on our unique path. Like any path or road, there are places where you can exit. These exits allow you to stop, refuel, or turn around. And just like the highway, there are times that we totally miss our off-ramp because we're not paying attention, and the sooner we realized that we missed it, the sooner we can catch the next one.

Anyone who has washed clothes in a clothes washing machine has known the rattle and noise that comes from the washing machine that is off-balance. And if you've witnessed the washing machine, when the clothes are clumped together on one side of the machine, the machine makes a thump, thump, thump. What is needed is for the machine to be paused or stopped, the lid to be opened, the clothes to be reset in the machine, the lid to be lowered, and the machine to be restarted.

In a convincing way, this is exactly what happens to you and me when we are rattling about, due to our own reaction to circumstances that are deemed pressure packed, demanding, or stressful.

The fact is, and it is my considered and experienced belief, that people operate more effectively (doing things that help) and reliably (not doing things that hinder) when responding from a calm, settled place—a place where one responds rather than reacts. This belief is rooted in my own experience and my experience witnessing others act with a mind full of racing thoughts, tension, and urgency, and watching it all crash and burn. This approach leads to apologies and regret, which creates a whole new situation to be anxious about.

Stress is part of life. The stress response is part of you. We've talked about how your story is really the only one that matters to you, because your story is the basis for how you react in certain situations—your stress response. Rampitude is about catching yourself earlier in your stress-response cycle. It's about acknowledging that you've been there before, it doesn't end well, and that you should pull off and reassess with a clear head. Rampitude is being aware that such off-ramps exist, and taking advantage of them. Remember, we are trainable, habits can form and habits can die, but it's up to us to develop them, and be really, really happy when it works.

Trust me, we can be the heroes we're supposed to be. But sometimes the best adventures begin with taking a step back.

My Friend John

This is the story of John. John is a really successful businessman, father, collegiate diver, world traveler, and *Thriving with Stress* participant. I met John a couple of years ago when he was going through the training. At the time he had a lot on his mind, but he listened, he took the training seriously, and I felt he was invested. John was attentive, and I did my best to help him understand his path, his response, and the framework. On the last day of his training, John and I shook hands, exchanged pleasantries, and parted ways.

A few months later John reached out to me, he wanted to meet for coffee and to talk. I happily accepted and met him the following week. I could sense that John had something on his mind, something he needed to get out. But in reality, I had no idea what he was about to tell me.

John was currently going through a messy divorce and an even messier custody battle. On the morning of the final custody hearing, John went to wake his daughter for school, like he always did. Only this time, his daughter said she wasn't going to school, she was going to court with him to tell the judge she wanted to live her mother. John calmly responded, "My job is to go to court, your job is to go to school."

That's it. He didn't yell, he didn't go on a tirade, he didn't even go into the next room and scream into a pillow.

John told me that without his training, he would've lost it, and rightfully so. On top of his divorce his daughter told him she doesn't want to be with him anymore, "losing it" doesn't even come close to what many of us would've done in John's position.

John recognized his stress response happening and chose to take an off-ramp. I don't tell you this story to brag (Okay, perhaps it's a little about bragging) but rather to demonstrate that if John can use his training in the Mt. Everest of stressful moments, using it when a coworker annoys us or our spouse isn't listening should be a piece of cake.

We can't change the stress, and we have no idea what type of stress is coming our way. We can only change the response, we can only change our role in the stress, and that's exactly what John did.

The Mind–Body Connection

We are entering uncharted but extremely important waters. The mind–body connection chapter is not for the faint of heart. Things are about to get real.

Actually, it's not that bad, but it is very important.

As we've already learned, there are four primary ways in which the human experiences stress: in his book *The Stress of Life*, endocrinologist Hans Selye noted the experience of stress includes (a) an increase in thoughts, (b) an increase in emotions, (c) an increase in body tension, and (d) an increase in pressured or forced behavior.

During a stress response you will experience all of these (thoughts, emotions, body tension, and pressured/reactive behavior).

I want you to imagine that the thoughts and emotions you experience are located in your mind. I honestly do not know exactly where your thoughts and or emotions are literally located—I'm not a wizard—but for the sake of the Rampitude framework, your thoughts and emotions are in your mind.

Our bodies experience tension and engage in behavior: pretty standard stuff, right? As you might imagine, during a stress response we experience increased thoughts, emotions, body tension, and pressured or reactive behavior. In the Rampitude framework, we call this a frustrated mind–body connection. It's frustrated because there is agitation in your thoughts, emotions, body tension, and pressured/reactive behavior.

Think about it like this: you're driving a car. An example of a normal mind–body connection (one that is not frustrated) is you think to yourself "I need to switch lanes" and so your body takes that thought, processes it, and the result is your left hand hitting the blinker while the right hand steers over to the adjacent lane.

Using this same scenario but with a stress response and a frustrated mind–body connection, the scenario changes. You reactively realize you need to switch lanes, you make your move, but someone cuts you off. This is where the stress response happens. Your heart rate increases, your mind races, your body responds by tightening your grip on the wheel, your foot moves to slam on the breaks. Once you know you're okay, your mind and body move from a place of survival to a place of anger. You bang your fist on the steering wheel, you yell, and perhaps give a hand gesture or two. Or, what's even worse, your frustration leads to speeding, which leads to getting pulled over.

Speaking of which, on the occasions in which we choose to take action when we have a frustrated mind–body connection, that is to say when we take action during a stress response, it often results in regret.

Regret usually means we have to apologize after an unnecessarily harsh response. And I think we can all agree, apologizing is the worst. Regret is so very common and often becomes part of relationships. It's not breaking up but making up that can, for some, become a really destructive habit.

I worked with one person who shared with me that he does not experience regret. Full disclosure: the man is a military trained force of nature. He did acknowledge that there are occasions when he feels the need to explain himself. For him, and perhaps you, the idea of "regret" is a sense that you did not perform at your best. I tell this story to remind people to not get hung up on the term "regret"—it means different things to different people.

In the world of marital therapy, a number of couples complain that the spouse squeezes the toothpaste tube in a way that's infuriating. And whether it is how a partner squeezes the toothpaste tube, or in the lack of engaged communication, most (if not all) arrived at this moment after years of unresolved frustration, or living day after day experiencing a frustrated mind–body connection while in a relationship.

Most faiths teach a lesson about not letting the sun go down on your anger. Personally, I think this is good advice because if you let days, weeks, months, years go down on your anger and you do not address the underlying issues, there will be a degree of death that will plague your relationship, your capacity, your stamina.

A life lived with an overriding Eeyore-like sense of regret—"Oh bother, another challenged reaction." Said another way, "Oh bother, here I go continuing to take action with a frustrated mind–body connection." That last one is if Eeyore was a stress expert.

The Stress Response and Rampitude

The purpose of introducing you to the Hero's Journey and the idea that there are these gateposts or off-ramps is to help you understand that you can get off the path earlier, no matter the path. And that if you get off of a path earlier, you are no longer on that path.

Simple, right?

To emphasize the value of Rampitude, here are some things that my friends, mentors, and colleagues have said about procrastinating in addressing your stress response.

HANS SELYE—It's not stress that kills you but your response to it: the end state of stress is death, to a relationship, to capacity, to tolerance.

(To learn more about Hans Selye, please visit his Wikipedia page - https://en.wikipedia.org/wiki/Hans_Selye)

ELISSA EPEL—"Damage induced by stress is usually due to the chronicity of exposure to the stress response. It often takes the form of a sluggish slow recovery from stress."

(To learn more about Elissa Epel, pleases visit her UCSF page - http://profiles.ucsf.edu/elissa.epel)

ROBERT SAPOLSKY—Dr. Sapolsky was in a National Geographic documentary titled *Stress: Portrait of a Killer,* which illustrates how prolonged exposure to stress can ruin your health in a multitude of ways. Dr. Sapolsky states in this documentary: *"Stress is not a state of mind. ... it's measurable and dangerous, and humans can't seem to find their off-switch."*

(To learn more about Robert Sapolsky, please visit his Wikipedia page - https://en.wikipedia.org/wiki /Robert_Sapolsky)

HERBERT BENSON—"60 to 90 percent of doctor visits are attributed to stress-related illnesses and symptoms."

(To learn more about Herbert Benson, please visit his Wikipedia page - https://en.wikipedia.org/wiki/Herbert_Benson)

STEVEN PORGES—"We evolved to eloquently transition from brief situations of danger to safety. However, when challenged by prolonged exposure to danger or by brief exposures to life threat, our nervous system may lose its resilience."

(To learn about Stephen Porges, please visit his Wikipedia page - https://en.wikipedia.org/wiki/Stephen_Porges)

RANDOM KID—I hate it when my parents fight.

(To learn more about random kids, talk to some of your neighbors)

In this book, we introduced you to the first 4 of the off-ramps used in the *Thriving with Stress* training: increased thoughts, increased emotions, increased body tension, and increased pressured behavior.

Each of these also occur when you experience a stress response. During a stress response you will experience an increase, most often when you are reacting to a demand in:

- **Thoughts**

- **Emotions**

- **Body tension**

- **Pressured or reactive behavior**

We learn to cover these implosions. "No, no, I am fine," says the manager about to break into tears over a new hire who realizes she made a major accounting error.

"No, no, I am fine," says the newly crowned manager who is tasked with managing direct reports who are his parents' age and who have more on-the-job experience.

Okay, let's do this together.

First, remember a time when you were under pressure, under a demand, or feeling stress. Do you have that memory fresh in your mind?

Now say with me, ready? "I am fine."

If you're like most, the words might sound a little hollow.

We've buried these implosions in the name of civility and social norms, despite the fact that *not* burying them would be absolutely fine.

When you bring your awareness to the experience of a stress response, you will begin to realize and identify the occasions in which they erupt inside you quicker than you previously had, if you identified these occasions at all. You may also experience this as an internal implosion inside you, like a volcano, and when you do, you'll have immediate, personal feedback that you're experiencing a stress response, courtesy of your body. You have a responsibility; you must pay attention to your experience, your rattle, your stress response. When you do, you will realize that you have a ready ability **to respond, not react**. When this happens, you will take a more flexible approach to the issue at hand and respond with greater effectiveness and greater reliability.

Do you remember how we learn and form new habits? Anytime you are developing a new skill, like noticing your mind–body connection and these first 4 off-ramps, this skill will come only in time and after a good bit of practice.

So today, this week, in the weeks to come, take a moment to notice these 4 indicators as you live your life today. What triggers them? How often? Take a good look at them and understand the role they play in your day-to-day life.

Wow, that was a lot to end a book. So now what?

Now that you have the Rampitude Framework and an understanding of the mind–body connection, you'll begin to notice how you feel when demands come your way. And when you do, you will soon realize that your mind and your body are your allies—ready to alert you when things are or seem dangerous.

At that moment, you are on the path.

Afterword

This is the end of our conversation for now. Rampitude is not about controlling, containing, denying, fighting, or avoiding the stress that comes your way. It's about gaining an ability to thrive, regardless of the demands that come.

Managing your stress response is a process. It takes time and effort, but it's worth it. You'll find that your relationships will be better, your outlook will be more positive, and you will be in control of your mind and your actions.

I encourage you to reach out with any questions or comments. After all, that's why I'm here.

—Dr. Frank Wood
www.thrivingwithstress.com
drfrank@thrivingwithstress.com

Read 👓 Write 👓 Share

In this final chapter we call Read – Write – Share, you have an opportunity to bring the reading of the book to life with your team. We include a section for you to comment on your experience in reading *Thriving with Stress*. As this book is intended to influence you and those around you, we invite you to share this book with others and when you do, we ask that you request that they (1) read the book (2) write their review in this section and (3) share the book with others. As directly as we can, we encourage you to reflect on your experience on your primary take away:

- Read the book

- Write your reflection

- Share this section of the book with others on your team so that they might read and write their reflections (do this in the squares that follow)

- Then come back together and share the experience as a team, division (or family)

We encourage you to be open to meeting. It is our experience that this bold step, being willing to meet, bears significant fruit. In fact, this simple decision can energize your team (or family) in a remarkable way. Consider using the following format:

1. Team manager gather the team (parent gather your partner and kids)

2. Read each reflection

3. Pause for 15 seconds after each

4. After each has been read, each person offers comment

5. Conclude the meeting

We hope that you learn and benefit from this framework on stress (and, more importantly, the importance of the stress-response life cycle) so that you might experience the confidence and freedom that comes when you THRIVE with the demands and pressures (the stress) that come with life with a sense of excitement at what might happen in your life, at work, at home and in your relationships!

Read 👓 Write 👓 Share

My Comments

_____

_____

_____

_____

_____

_____

_____

_____

_____

My Comments

_____

_____

_____

_____

_____

_____

_____

_____

_____

My Comments

_____

_____

_____

_____

_____

_____

_____

_____

_____

My Comments

_____

_____

_____

_____

_____

_____

_____

_____

_____

My Comments

_____

_____

_____

_____

_____

_____

_____

_____

_____

My Comments

_____

_____

_____

_____

_____

_____

_____

_____

_____

My Comments

_____

_____

_____

_____

_____

_____

_____

_____

_____

My Comments

_____

_____

_____

_____

_____

_____

_____

_____

_____

My Comments

My Comments

Dr. Frank, founder and CEO of *Thriving with Stress*, developed an innovative training program to leverage stress—in the workplace, relationships and life. Born in Jefferson County, KY, grandson of a two-star general, he is a father of three, loyal friend, and Sudoku master.

An invited speaker, author and trainer on stress, Dr. Frank has a PhD in Clinical Psychology, and has invested more than 10 years in practice. Over time, and with careful study, Dr. Frank has applied all of his expertise and experience in developing the Thriving with Stress program, a program that clients refer to as a "game changer" and a "program that is turning the tables on stress."

Dr. Frank shares his fresh perspective on stress both in this book and at the TEDxUCincinnati with the topic **The WHY of Stress**. In both, he shares his framework for the commonly misunderstood topic of stress.

Also in 2016, Dr. Frank will launch the inaugural digital format of his training, **Thriving with Stress: Your Resilient Divorce**.

Made in the USA
San Bernardino, CA
20 February 2016